OLE EVINRUDE
and His Outboard Motor

Other Badger Biographies

OLE EVINRUDE

and His Outboard Motor

BOB JACOBSON

WISCONSIN HISTORICAL SOCIETY PRESS

Published by the Wisconsin Historical Society Press
Publishers since 1855

© 2009 by State Historical Society of Wisconsin

For permission to reuse material from *Ole Evinrude and His Outboard Motor*, ISBN 978-0-87020-420-3, please access www.copyright.com or contact the Copyright Clearance Center, Inc. (CCC), 222 Rosewood Drive, Danvers, MA 01923, 978-750-8400. CCC is a not-for-profit organization that provides licenses and registration for a variety of users.

wisconsin**history**.org

Photographs identified with PH, WHi, or WHS are from the Society's collections; address requests to reproduce these photos to the Visual Materials Archivist at the Wisconsin Historical Society, 816 State Street, Madison, WI 53706.

Printed in the United States of America
Designed by Jill Bremigan

13 12 11 10 09   1 2 3 4 5

Library of Congress Cataloging-in-Publication Data

Jacobson, Bob, 1963–
   Ole Evinrude and his outboard motor / Bob Jacobson.
      p. cm.—(Badger biographies series)
   Includes bibliographical references and index.
   ISBN 978-0-87020-420-3 (pbk. : alk. paper)
1. Evinrude, Ole, 1877–1934. 2. Outboard motors—History—Juvenile literature. 3. Inventors—United States—Biography—Juvenile literature. 4. Businessmen—Wisconsin—Biography—Juvenile literature. 5. Norwegian Americans—Wisconsin—Biography—Juvenile literature. I. Title.
   VM348.J33 2008
   338.7'62387234092—dc22
   [B]
                              2008030790

Front cover: Norwegian Emigrant Museum
Back cover: WHi Image ID 36551

∞ The paper used in this publication meets the minimum requirements of the American National Standard for Information Sciences—Permanence of Paper for Printed Library Materials, ANSI Z39.48-1992.

This book is dedicated to the generations of immigrants from all over the world who have settled in Wisconsin in search of a better life for their children and grandchildren. Some of them, like Ole Evinrude, have left a lasting mark in business, science, or some other field. Most of them have lived quieter lives but have nevertheless contributed in a huge way to their communities. It is those people and their families who give Wisconsin its special flavor, making it a great place to live, visit, or just putter around in a motorboat.

Publication of this book was made possible, in part, by a gift from Mrs. Harvey E. Vick of Milwaukee, Wisconsin.

Contents

1

Meet Ole Evinrude

When people hear the name Thomas Edison, they instantly think of the lightbulb. **Ole Evinrude** may not be as famous as Edison, but to people who love boats, his name is just as familiar. If you've ever puttered across a lake in a small motorized boat, you have Ole to thank. Ole loved boats. He helped make **outboard motors** a common sight on Wisconsin lakes. Little did he know that the idea he had one hot summer day to put a motor on a boat would make his name and Wisconsin famous for outboard motors.

Ole Evinrude was born on April 19, 1877, on a farm about 60 miles from Christiana, the largest city in Norway. Christiana's name was changed to Oslo soon after Ole was born. Oslo is still Norway's biggest city and its capital.

Ole Evinrude (**oh** lee **ev** in rude)   **outboard motor**: a motor attached to the outside of a boat

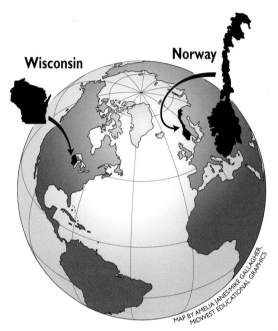

MAP BY AMELIA JANES/MIKE GALLAGHER, MIDWEST EDUCATIONAL GRAPHICS

Ole was born on a farm near Christiana, the largest city in Norway.

Ole was the oldest boy among his parents' 11 children. His father, Andrew, was a **strict** and practical man who worked hard to make a living running the family farm. Ole's mother, Beatta, was a gentle, quiet woman who came from a long line of **blacksmiths** and metalworkers. Perhaps it was from Beatta's side of the family, the Dahls, that Ole **inherited** his **engineering** skills. Ole's earliest memories of Norway were of the lake near the Evinrude farm. He loved to play on its shore and watch the boats go by.

When Ole was 5 years old, the Evinrude family moved to America in search of a better life. Even at that young age, Ole's fascination with boats and engines was obvious. He spent as much of the trip across the Atlantic Ocean as possible in

strict: making someone follow all the rules **blacksmith**: someone who makes and fits horseshoes and other things made of iron **inherited** (in **hair** i did): received a skill or quality passed down from parents
engineering (en juh **neer** ring): having to do with engines and engine design

2

the ship's engine room. He loved to watch the giant engines do their work. His mother and grandmother considered the engine room an unsafe place for a small child. They spent the entire trip dragging him out of the engine room, only to have him wander back at the first opportunity.

Ole came to America on a ship like this. This ship, the *Bergensfjord,* was part of the Norwegian America Line.

The dining room onboard the immigrant ship *Bergensfjord.*

The deck of the ship that brought Ole to America looked something like this.

Arriving in America, the Evinrudes settled on a farm in Cambridge, Wisconsin, near Lake Ripley. Ole's education in America was divided between the old and the new. For 8 months of each year, his schooling was in English. He attended a Norwegian school for another 3 months. This may sound like a lot of school—most kids in America today get the whole summer off—but Ole didn't stick around for long. He left school after finishing third grade. By that time, however, he could already do the math that was usually given to eighth graders. Actually, it was pretty common for kids to leave school early in those days. Many children worked on their families'

This wheat farm was in a Norwegian community close to Cambridge where Ole lived.

A dairy farm in Christiana Township in Dane County around 1875. Christiana Township was named after the town in Norway that Ole's family came from.

4

farms and did not go to school at all (even though Wisconsin had a law requiring that all children ages 7 to 14 attend school for at least 12 weeks a year).

Although Norwegians have a long history of sailing and boatbuilding, Ole's father, Andrew, wanted nothing to do with either. Three of Andrew's uncles had been lost at sea back in Norway. He saw the **seafaring** life as dangerous compared to the relative safety of farming. He wanted his son Ole to follow in his footsteps as a farmer. But boatbuilding seemed to be in Ole's blood. One of his uncles was a sailor who had been all over the world. He would sometimes visit Ole's family in Wisconsin in between his adventures on the sea. Ole loved hearing his uncle's tales. From his uncle, Ole also learned all about the different types of boats and ships.

As Ole got older, he was given more responsibilities on the farm. By the time he was 10 years old, he was working alongside his father in the fields full-time. He quickly showed a talent with tools. He was often able to fix things on the spot that normally would have required a trip to the blacksmith shop in town. During the winter, when he was not helping

seafaring: working at sea

his father on the farm, Ole worked as a **sorter** in the nearby tobacco warehouses. Ole used his money from that job to buy a subscription to a magazine about **mechanical** science. Ole loved to try out the engineering knowledge he gained from the magazine around the farm. He would spend hours **tinkering** with his father's farm equipment. He tried to find ways to improve the way the equipment worked.

But farm equipment was not Ole's true love. What he loved most of all was boatbuilding. When he was 15,

Ole worked on a tobacco farm like this one in the winter.

Ole started building his first boat. He knew his father would not approve of this activity, so Ole had to keep the project carefully hidden in the woodshed. One day, Andrew discovered the partially built boat. In a fit of rage he smashed the boat to

sorter: a person who arranges things in groups   **mechanical** (muh **kan** i kuhl): having to do with machines
tinkering: making repairs without being an expert

pieces and threw them into the woodstove. Ole was crushed by his father's action. A lot of people may have given up after such a disappointment. But Ole Evinrude was not the kind of person to abandon his dream so easily.

After Andrew destroyed the boat, Ole simply started building another one. He didn't want to disobey his father, but the urge to build a boat was **overwhelming**. This time, he found better hiding places for the boat parts. He hid the pieces in different places around the farm. Ole figured that even if his father found one of the pieces, he wouldn't be able to tell that it was part of a boat being built.

WHI IMAGE ID 39612

Many people liked to go boating on Lake Ripley.

overwhelming: having a strong effect

7

Working at odd hours whenever he could find the time, Ole finally finished building his 18-foot sailboat. He put it in the water and waited anxiously to see how his father would react. To Ole's surprise, his father did not get mad. Andrew simply said, "I'd hoped to make a farmer out of you, but I guess you're cut out for something better, son. You've built a right nice boat."

PH 490

WISCONSIN

LAKE RIPLEY

As a boy Ole Evinrude (1877-1934) lived near Cambridge. His father hoped to keep him on the farm and when Ole built a sailboat like he had seen in a picture book his father destroyed it. In a secret place in the woods the boy built another. Here on Lake Ripley, as his father watched from shore Ole sailed the well-built craft with all the instinctive skill of his Viking ancestors. Soon after, he left for the city to work as a mechanic. In 1908 he invented the outboard motor and founded a new American industry.

A historical marker was dedicated to Ole in 1955.

Once he had won his father's approval, Ole was ready to put his new boat to work. That summer, he charged **sightseers** 25 cents to ferry them around on Lake Ripley. Customers kept him busy on the lake all day on some weekends. When the weather was nice, Ole could earn as much as $5 on a Sunday. That was quite a lot of money in those days. You could buy about as much for $5 back then as you can buy for $100 today.

sightseer: a visitor

2

Ole the Engineer

When the summer he was 15 came to an end, Ole became restless. With his parents' permission, he moved to Madison, the capital of Wisconsin. Madison is about 20 miles from Cambridge. In Madison, Ole was an **apprentice** at the Fuller and Johnson farm machinery shop. It was a good thing that Ole had made so much money giving boat rides over the summer. His room and board in Madison cost $3.50 per week, but he was paid only $2.50 per week at his apprentice job. He also had enough money left over to continue his science magazine subscription. The magazine sparked his imagination with its articles about new engines that ran on a new kind of fuel called "gasoline" rather than on steam. Ole worked about 10 hours a day at the

Madison ★ • Milwaukee
Cambridge •

MAP BY JOEL HEIMAN

apprentice (uh **pren** tis): someone who works for a set amount of time for low pay in return for being taught the skills of a trade

9

shop. After he returned to his **boarding house**, he spent hours more reading everything he could get his hands on about engineering,

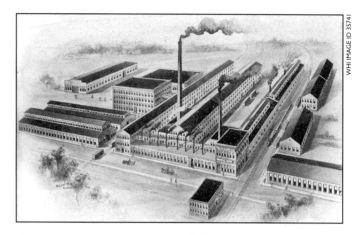

Ole was an apprentice at the Fuller and Johnson Company in Madison.

math, and mechanics.

As an apprentice, Ole learned his craft well, and he was soon ready to launch a career as a **machinist**. He worked in several other machine shops in Madison, including one that made electric motors. For the next 5 years, Ole bounced from one job to another, learning everything he needed to know in order to become a mechanical engineer. From Madison, Ole moved to Pittsburgh, Pennsylvania, the heart of America's steel industry. In Pittsburgh, Ole found work in the steel-rolling mills. These mills turn plain slabs of steel into steel sheets or coils that can be used in **manufacturing**. At the mill, he learned

boarding house: a house that provides meals and rents rooms to live in   **machinist** (muh **shee** nist): somebody who makes, operates, or fixes machines   **manufacturing:** (man yoo **fak** shur ring): making a product with the use of a machine

the finer points of **metallurgy**. When he decided that he had
learned enough about rolling steel, Ole moved back to the
Midwest and settled in Chicago. There he landed a series
of jobs that helped him to master the art of machine tool
making. Machine tools are power-driven tools, such as a **lathe**
or drill, used to cut or shape raw material into a usable form.
Along the way, he also learned how to draw detailed machine
plans and how to make models from the drawings. This skill
is known as pattern making.

WHI IMAGE ID 9761

This machine shop has lathes and other power-driven tools.

metallurgy (**met** uh lur jee): the science of working with metal   **lathe** (layth): a machine that holds a piece of
metal or wood while turning it against a cutting tool that shapes it

In 1900, when Ole was 23 years old, he returned to Wisconsin. He lived in Milwaukee, where he got a job running the pattern-making shop of the E. P. Allis Company. The E. P. Allis Company was a major manufacturing company that made, among other things, steam engines. But Ole had a new interest that took up most of his spare time. He had read about a new type of engine called the **internal combustion engine**—the kind of engine that powers automobiles. Ole began spending every free moment he had working on his own internal combustion engine. He was sure that he could use all the engineering knowledge he had gained to make his own automobile.

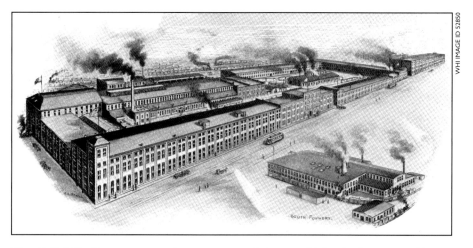

The E. P. Allis Company was known around the world for its large machinery.

internal combustion (kuhm **bus** chuhn) **engine**: a type of engine in which fuel is burned inside an enclosed space in the engine rather than in an outside furnace

In Milwaukee, Ole lived in a boarding house owned by a woman named Mrs. Doyle. It was in the basement of Mrs. Doyle's house that Ole built his first engine. The day his engine was ready to try out, Ole forgot to buy gasoline. So that night he hooked the engine up to the pipe in the basement that supplied gas to all of the lights in Mrs. Doyle's house. Ole

Ole at his drawing table, where he could almost always be found.

cranked the engine. It worked perfectly! The engine sprang to life with an earsplitting roar. It also used all of the gas coming from the pipe. The entire house **plunged** briefly into darkness. Not suprisingly, the guests at Mrs. Doyle's dinner party that evening were somewhat startled. After that, Mrs. Doyle kindly asked Ole not to cause any more explosions in her basement.

plunged (pluhnjd): moved suddenly

Ole set out in search of a new place to tinker with his engine. He soon found a shed for rent next to the property of a young woman named Bess Cary. Her father had died the year before. Now she was taking classes at the local business college so that she would be able to help support the family. Bess was only 16 years old.

Ole continued to improve his engine designs over the next few years. He eventually did manage to build his own automobile. He attached a small engine to a **carriage**. It was loud and put out enough smoke to fill the entire street. But it was also strange and exciting enough to draw crowds of people whenever Ole took it out for a spin. It was a good thing that it drew crowds, since it broke down quite often. Ole often needed help pushing it back to the shop.

Ole hoped to start a company to make and sell his automobile. He realized, however, that he would need a partner in order to make it happen. He formed a company with a fellow machinist named Clark. But neither Ole nor Clark had **marketing** skills, so they quickly went their separate ways. A few months later, Ole found a new partner.

carriage: a cart with wheels   **marketing**: selling products or services

They formed a company called Clemick and Evinrude. This new company designed and built **custom** engines and parts for other companies to use in their manufacturing. This company was quite successful at first. The partners received an order from the United States government for 50 **portable** engines. Several car makers—which seemed to be springing up everywhere—also bought engines from Clemick and Evinrude. After only a few months in business, the company was making its products in 6 different machine shops in Milwaukee. They hired Ole's neighbor Bess to take care of the company's **bookkeeping** and marketing. Ole enjoyed spending time with Bess very much.

Unfortunately, after such a great start, things started to sour for Clemick and Evinrude. The 2 partners could not agree on how to run the company. The company fell apart after only 6 months. Next, Ole formed a new company called the Motor Car Power Equipment Company, in **partnership** with a retired furniture dealer. Again, the company quickly collapsed, because the partner foolishly refused to spend any money on advertising.

custom: made or built to order **portable**: able to be moved or carried easily **bookkeeping**: keeping track of money **partnership**: a business agreement between 2 or more people

All of these failed partnerships may make it seem as though Ole was just a bad businessman. But it was more complicated than that. The end of the 1800s and beginning of the 1900s was an amazing period of change in the history of inventions and manufacturing. Exciting new machines were showing up every year. Inventors and **entrepreneurs** fiercely competed for the public's attention.

Throughout this period of failed partnerships, Ole continued to work hard trying to make an automobile that was good enough to put on the market. He eventually developed a car he called the Eclipse. Once again he found partners to start manufacturing and selling the Eclipse. Once again he didn't get along with them, and the **venture** crumbled. That was really unfortunate, because there was nothing wrong with the car that Ole had designed. If he had had better luck (or better skill) at choosing business partners, it's quite possible that Ole Evinrude could have become a pioneer in the automobile industry, like Henry Ford! Instead, after 4 disappointing business failures, Ole gave up on his dream of making and selling automobiles.

entrepreneur (on truh pruh **nur**): a person who risks his or her money to start a business   **venture**: a project that could be risky

Key Inventions Around the Turn of the Century

An incredible number of important new inventions were created around the turn of the twentieth century. Here are just a few of them:

Year	Invention	Inventor
1891	Modern escalator	Jesse W. Reno
1893	Zipper	Whitcomb L. Judson
1895	Diesel engine	Rudolf Diesel
1895	Radio signals	Guglielmo Marconi
1898	Remote control	Nikola Tesla
1899	Magnetic tape recorder	Valdemar Poulsen
1901	Vacuum cleaner	Hubert Booth
1902	Air conditioner	Willis Carrier
1903	Powered airplane	Wilbur and Orville Wright
1907	Helicopter	Paul Cornu

Automobile Time Line

Ole designed an automobile called the Eclipse in the early 1900s, but history pretty much forgot about his car. Here are some key events and dates in the early development of the automobile that history has not forgotten:

Model T

1876 — Nikolaus Otto builds the first 4-cycle internal combustion engine.

1885 — Karl Benz builds the first successful motor vehicle, a 3-wheeled cycle powered by a gasoline engine.

1886 — Gottfried Daimler builds the first modern automobile.

1901 — The Olds automobile factory opens in Detroit.

1908 — William Durant founds General Motors.

1908 — Henry Ford introduces the Model T.

1913 — Ford Motor Company introduces the first moving **assembly line** for manufacturing automobiles.

assembly line: an arrangement of machines and workers in which work passes from one worker to the next until the product is finished

3

Romance + Ice Cream = An Idea

While Ole was having a terrible time with his business partners, he was having much better luck getting along with a different kind of partner. Throughout his series of failed partnerships, Bess Cary stuck with Ole as his bookkeeper and all-around business assistant. Over time, their relationship grew beyond just business. They become close friends, and before long they began to fall in love.

Discouraged after the failure of his car company, Ole went back to the job he knew best: pattern making.

Bess Evinrude. Ole and Bess were partners at work and at home.

19

He opened his own pattern-making shop in a rented space on the city's south side above a **forge** owned by a man named John Obenberger. By this time, Ole had an excellent **reputation** as a pattern maker, so he had plenty of customers for his new shop. Business was so good that at times he had as many as 6 pattern makers working for him in the little shop.

And now for the ice cream story. This story may be true, partly true, or completely made up. In any case, the ice cream story stuck because it's a pretty good story to tell.

One Sunday in August of 1906, Ole, Bess, and a couple of friends went on a picnic. They rowed to a nice picnic spot across Lake **Okauchee**, west of Milwaukee. It was a very hot day. According to the story, after lunch Bess said that she would really like some ice cream. So Ole, eager to please his future wife, hopped into the boat. He rowed about 2½ miles to Shatz's ice cream parlor on the other side of the lake. Naturally, by the time he rowed all the way back to the picnic site in the hot summer sun, the ice cream had melted. Ole's friends thought it was pretty funny, but Ole was mad. Then suddenly, an idea popped into his head: why not invent a

forge (forj): a metal workshop **reputation** (rep yoo **tay** shuhn): the opinion that people have about something or someone **Okauchee**: oh **kaw** chee

motor that you could stick right onto the back of a rowboat so that you could bring ice cream to your girlfriend before it all melted?

Ole may have thought up his outboard motor after rowing miles to bring ice cream to his girlfriend Bess.

Like many great ideas, this one took awhile to ripen. Ole had other things to do before he could work on his new invention. For starters, he had to marry Bess, the woman who had inspired him to think up the outboard motor. Ole and Bess were married in a small ceremony on November 21, 1906. Ole would later describe his wedding as "the one ray of light that pierced the gloom" created by his series of business failures. The couple did not wait long to start a family. Their only child, Ralph Evinrude, was born on September 27, 1907.

Ole may not have known it at the time, but several other people before him had already thought of attaching a motor to a rowboat. The first gasoline-powered outboard motor that anybody seems to remember was made 10 years earlier, in 1896, by the American Motors Company (not to be confused with the later car company with the same name) of Long Island City, New York. That outboard motor didn't work very well. Several other people tried to make outboard motors over the next several years, but most of those didn't work well either.

The only outboard motor before Ole's that was successful was called the "Porto." It was designed in 1906 by a man named Cameron Waterman. Waterman lived near Detroit, Michigan. Detroit is famous for being the birthplace of the car industry. It was a natural place for somebody to come up with a design for a different kind of engine. Waterman sold 3,000 of his Porto motors in 1907, and his company continued to make them for another 10 years. The Porto worked okay but not well enough to become very popular.

Meanwhile, the Evinrudes were struggling. Ralph's birth had been difficult for Bess, and her health was poor for a long time afterward. The family was also struggling **financially**. Ole was putting in very long hours at his shop and barely sleeping. He began to have health problems as well. He suffered from

financially (fɪ **nan** shuh lee): having to do with money

rheumatism. When he was too sick to go to the shop, he had his drawing board brought to his bed, and he worked from there.

One day in 1909, Ole's hard work finally paid off. He managed to build his first outboard motor! Ole's motor was

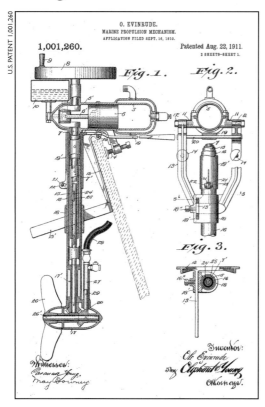

different from—and better than—any of the others that had been built before. In fact, Ole's outboard motor was so good that the basic design has hardly changed at all since then. Think about it: nobody has figured out how to make one that works much better in 100 years! Newer models are lighter, quieter, more powerful, and start easier, but the basic idea is pretty much the same.

Ole's first **patent** for an outboard motor.

rheumatism (**roo** muh tiz uhm): a painful condition of the muscles and joints   **patent** (**pat** uhnt): a legal document that gives an inventor all of the rights to an invention

23

What's an Outboard Motor? How Does It Work?

An outboard motor is a motor that you attach to the outside of a boat to make it go. Outboard motors work a lot like other small motors, such as those found on lawn mowers or motorbikes. While some outboard motors are powered by electricity, most of them run on gasoline, just like a car engine. Gasoline-powered outboard motors are louder than electric ones, but they are also more powerful. Like car engines, gasoline-powered outboard motors are based on a type of engine called an internal combustion engine. "Internal" means inside, and "combustion" means burning. So putting them together, it means a type of engine that works by burning gasoline inside of it. In an internal combustion engine, gasoline is burned inside of a small enclosed space, or chamber, in a series of small explosions. Each little explosion makes the gases inside the chamber expand, and this pressure pushes on a part called a piston. As the piston moves up and down, it moves a series of rods, rotors, and other parts that make the motor rotate in circles.

Most outboard motors are "2-stroke" engines. That means that each explosion makes the piston go down (the first stroke) and then back up (the second stroke) once, resulting in one full turn of the motor. In an outboard motor, this motion turns a propeller, which sits just below the surface of the water. The outboard motor is attached to the stern, or back, of the boat. So the spinning of the propeller pushes the boat through the water. Outboard motors usually have a handle attached to them. This allows a person sitting in the back of the boat to turn the motor so that it pushes the boat in the right direction. The part of the motor that goes below the surface of the water also acts as a rudder. A rudder is how you steer a boat with an outboard motor.

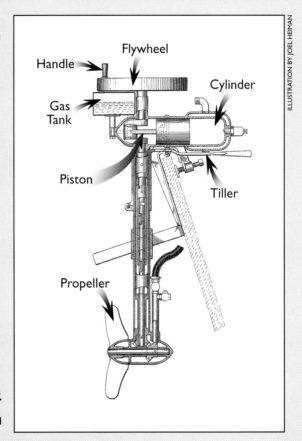

ILLUSTRATION BY JOEL HEIMAN

A look inside an outboard motor.

25

At first, Bess thought her husband's **contraption** looked like a coffee grinder. She was angry at Ole for wasting so much time on such a silly project. But she changed her mind once she found out how well it worked. Ole and Russ Cary, Bess's brother, carried the motor to the nearby **Kinnickinnic** River and attached it to a rowboat they had rented. They started up the motor. It was very loud, but it worked perfectly! Now Bess believed in Ole's new invention. She encouraged him to clean up the design and make it look better. So Ole polished up the brass, painted some parts, and added a **muffler** to make it quieter. He then ordered enough parts to make 25 of the motors. He figured he might be able to sell that many during the summer.

One Sunday soon after that, Ole had one of his workers take the motor to **Pewaukee** Lake for a **demonstration**. By the time the worker returned to the shop the next day, he had sold the motor he had with him and had taken orders for 10 more of them! Ole built the 10 engines himself. They weighed 62 pounds each and sold for $62—a dollar per pound, just like something you'd buy at the supermarket!

contraption (kuhn **trap** shuhn): a device or machine   **Kinnickinnic: kin** ik kin ik   **muffler:** a part that lessens engine noise   **Pewaukee:** pee **wah** kee   **demonstration:** a showing of how to do something

That summer—the summer of 1909—Bess wrote a **slogan** to appear in ads they placed in the Milwaukee newspapers. The ads said: "DON'T ROW! THROW THE OARS AWAY! USE AN EVINRUDE MOTOR!" The people of Milwaukee must have been ready to throw away their oars. Almost as soon as the ads appeared, the remaining 15 of Ole's first batch of motors were sold.

Evinrude outboard motors were an instant hit. Orders flooded in faster than Ole could fill them. In 1910, Ole borrowed money from a business **associate** so that he could move into a bigger shop at

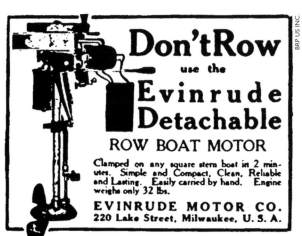

This ad brought a flood of orders for Evinrude motors.

228 Lake Street, just a few doors down from the old one. That year, the company received nearly 1,000 orders for outboard motors. By this time there were about 100 people working in the shop. Bess and her sister Dorothy handled all of the office

slogan: a phrase used by a business to sell something   **associate** (uh **soh** see it): a person involved in the company

duties. When Bess placed ads for the motors nationwide, they had to hire 6 more office workers within 3 days just to handle all of the new orders that came pouring in.

Bess's advertisements were almost *too* successful. The business was growing faster than she and Ole could keep up!

Bess turned "Evinrude" into a verb in this ad.

They needed a bigger factory to stay on top of the flood of orders, but they didn't have the money to buy a bigger building or more equipment. So Ole began to look for a business partner who had enough money necessary to make the business bigger. In 1911, an old customer of Ole's named Chris Meyer, who was president of Meyer Tug Boat Lines, gave Ole $5,000 for half of the new outboard business.

28

He became equal partners with Ole. Together, they formed the Evinrude **Detachable** Row Boat Motor Company.

Now Ole could move the company into a larger space. The partners found a 3-story building on Reed Street that had been a soap factory. They were now able to meet the growing demand for outboard motors. In 1911, the new, improved Evinrude company sold more than 2,000 motors. The outboard motor was no longer just some silly **gadget** that looked a little like a coffee grinder; it was a useful machine that people seemed to love!

detachable (di **tach** uh buhl): a part that separates from something else   **gadget** (**gaj** it): a tool or part that does a particular job

4

Building a Better Motor

One problem with making your living from boats is that it is a **seasonal** business. It is much better at certain times of the year than others. In some parts of the United States, including Wisconsin, there are a few months when it is too cold to use boats and the lakes are covered in ice. Ole and Bess had to find a way to deal with the fact that sales were going to slow down during the winter. It was Bess who came up with a solution to this problem. She began to contact **export companies** in New York to see if it might be possible to start selling Evinrude outboard motors outside of the United States.

Most of the companies Bess contacted ignored her letters. But one **agent** saw that the motors might prove to be popular among **Scandinavian** fishermen. Scandinavia is the part of northern Europe that includes the countries of Norway, Sweden, and Denmark. This agent ordered a small number of

seasonal: happening during the spring, summer, fall, or winter   **export company**: a company that sends products to other countries   **agent** (**ay** juhnt): a person who represents a business   **Scandinavian** (scan di **nay** vee uhn)

motors to be demonstrated in those 3 countries. The agent was right. Evinrude outboard motors were a big hit in Scandinavia. His demonstration quickly resulted in an order for 1,000 motors.

Ole liked to test his inventions himself. Here he is on the lake with a newly designed engine.

In 1912 the company sold 4,650 motors, doubling its yearly total once again. The company moved again, too, into an even bigger space, this time on Walker Street. But even this new factory proved to be too small. The next year, 1913, sales doubled yet again, reaching 9,412 motors. About 300 employees worked in the newest factory. By this time, the name Evinrude was becoming well known among boating fans all over the world. Ole managed the Evinrude factory and served as its chief engineer. Bess was in charge of the company's advertising and **public relations**. She generally kept the office running smoothly. The company was zooming along, but the long hours were again beginning

public relations: activities used to create a good reputation with the public

to wear Ole and Bess down. They hadn't had a vacation in 4 years. Bess had never recovered her full strength after her son's birth. She began to suffer from some health problems. And she and Ole didn't have nearly enough time to spend with Ralph, who was now 6 years old.

With the business going well, Ole and Bess decided that it didn't need them anymore. In 1914 Ole sold his half of the Evinrude Detachable Row Boat Motor Company to his partner, Chris Meyer, for $137,500. That may sound like a lot of money now, but in 1914 it was worth quite a lot more! It would take about $2.5 million today to buy as much stuff as $137,500 could buy in 1914. As part of the deal, Ole agreed to stay out of the outboard motor business for the next 5 years.

Employees of the Evinrude factory, 1916.

Now free to spend their time as they pleased, the Evinrude family started a new life of **leisure**. They bought

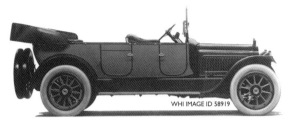

The Evinrudes traveled America in a Packard touring car something like this one.

a Packard **touring car** and loaded it with lots of outdoor sports equipment. After years of working harder than was good for them, the Evinrudes set out to explore America. They travelled for a while by land, and then the Evinrudes went south. They bought a **cabin cruiser** and started exploring the Florida coast by sea. Six months later, the family returned to Milwaukee, where they toured the Great Lakes on a 42-foot cruiser designed by Ole called the *Bess Emily*. When they'd had enough of the Great Lakes, they cruised down the Mississippi River in the fall of 1917 to spend the winter in New Orleans, Louisiana. Gradually, all of this relaxation helped both Bess and Ole **regain** their health and strength. By the time they reached New Orleans, Ole had gotten an idea for a new and improved version of his outboard motor. He decided that he'd had quite enough of a rest. Ole was ready to get back to work.

leisure (**lee** zhur): free time when you don't have to work   **touring car**: a car made for driving long distances
cabin cruiser: a type of boat with living quarters   **regain**: to get something back

33

Meanwhile, Ole's old company was struggling under Chris Meyer's leadership. The company had made a few minor improvements in the design of the Evinrude outboard motor, but each year they were selling fewer of them. From the 9,412 motors the company sold under Ole and Bess in 1913, sales dropped to 7,180 in 1914, 6,222 in 1915, and 5,534 in 1917. Despite these shrinking numbers, Evinrude remained the world's leading outboard motor producer.

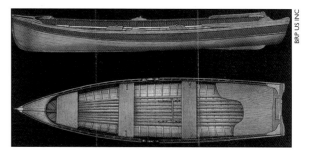

Evinrude also made round bottom boats like these in the late 1910s and early 1920s.

During this period, Ole could not go back into the outboard motor business because of his agreement with Meyer. But that did not stop him from thinking about outboard motors. By 1919, the end of his agreement, Ole had come up with a **revolutionary** new design. Ole's new motor was made largely of **aluminum**. Aluminum is much lighter than the bronze, steel, and iron used in the Evinrude engine.

revolutionary (rev uh **loo** shuhn air ree): a large, important change   **aluminum** (uh **loo** mi nuhm)

The new motor weighed only 42 pounds. It was also about 50 percent more powerful than the earlier Evinrude model.

RALPH LAMBRECHT

Elto motors weighed less than earlier models. The company thought this would be more appealing to women.

With plans for his new engine in hand, Ole visited Meyer. He wanted to discuss working with his old company to produce the new motor. To Ole's surprise, Meyer was not interested. He was still making money from the old engine, and he saw no reason to form a new partnership. Ole, however, was certain that the new engine was much better than the old one. He decided to start his own company. His new company would **compete** directly with the company that had his name.

compete (kuhm **peet**): to try hard to outdo someone at something

So in 1920, Ole and Bess started a new company from scratch. They could not use their own name, Evinrude, for the new company's name, because Meyer alone owned the right to use it for business. They settled on the name Elto Outboard

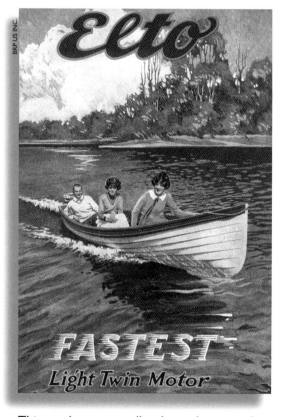

Motor Company. Bess came up with the name Elto by combining the first letters of the phrase Evinrude Light Twin Outboard. With about $35,000 in savings, they rented shop space, bought some used equipment, and went to work producing the Elto motor. As before, Ole ran the shop while Bess managed the office.

This catalog cover talks about the motor's speed, but the boat does not look like it's going fast enough to mess up the passengers' hair!

By the time the Elto company was formed, there was a lot more competition in the outboard motor business. As a result, Elto lost money in its first year. But slowly the company grew more successful. In 1921, Ole and Bess sold about 1,000 Elto motors. The following year, the number of motors sold reached 2,500. That was more than the old Evinrude company managed to sell that year. In 1922, Chris Meyer sold the Evinrude company.

By this time, however, another company had jumped into the lead in the outboard motor industry. The Johnson Motor Company, based in South Bend, Indiana, had begun making motors that performed better than the old Evinrudes. The biggest Evinrude and Elto motors in 1926 were 4 horsepower. Horsepower is the unit of measurement used to describe how powerful a machine is. Johnson's motor was 6 horsepower and getting more powerful every year. Around this time, boat racing was becoming a popular sport. Johnson was the first company to give racing customers faster, more powerful motors.

What Is Horsepower?

You've probably heard the word horsepower before. Most ads for cars, lawn mowers, and motorcycles tell you about the machine's horsepower. Horsepower is a way of measuring the power of an engine. The word was created by engineer James Watt in the 1700s. He wanted a way to talk about the power available from horses lifting coal from a coal mine. One horsepower is equal to one horse moving 330 pounds of coal 100 feet in one minute. This unit of measure made its way down through the centuries and is now used to show how much work a machine can accomplish or how fast it can **accelerate**.

But Ole worked hard to keep up with Johnson, and the Elto company **prospered**. He spent a lot of money on advertising and managed to sell about 7,600 Elto motors by 1925. Johnson was the only company that sold more. In 1926, Elto introduced a new 2-cylinder motor (remember, the cylinders in a motor are the chambers in which the fuel is burned) called the Super Elto Twin. It proved to be quite popular. Not to be **outdone**, the Johnson company kept

accelerate (ak **sel** uh rate): to get faster and faster   prospered (pros purd): to be successful
outdone: done better than

38

building faster and more powerful motors. These motors set new world speed records in 1925 and 1926. Ole fought back with the first 4-cylinder outboard motor ever offered, the 92–pound, 18-horsepower Elto High Speed Quad. The Quad sold for $275. It was the first in a string of 4-cylinder motors that would grow in power over the next several years, reaching 40 horsepower in 1930 and peaking at 50 horsepower in 1946. Outboard racing was becoming a popular **spectator sport** in some parts of the country, including the Midwest, in the late 1920s. The Quad was the engine of choice for many top racers. In 1928, the year the Quad was **launched**, Elto sold more than 10,000 motors and made more than $300,000.

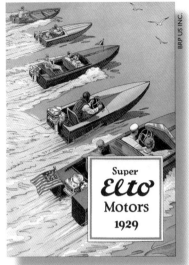

A 1929 Elto catalog.

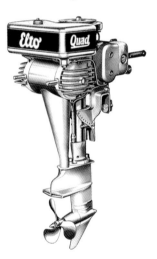

The 1929 Elto Quad was the first 4-cylinder outboard motor.

spectator sport: a sport watched by an audience   **launched** (lawnchd): introduced something new

39

5

A Captain of Industry

Ole Evinrude came from a **generation** of immigrants who made their own way in the world without much education. Ole's formal education had ended in third grade. Even so, over the years, he managed to educate himself in all of the subjects he needed to be successful in engineering and in business. But immigrants who did well in the United States expected something better for their children. Unlike Ole himself, Ole's son, Ralph, didn't have to worry about earning a living as a young man. His father was happy to support him while he finished college. That's exactly what Ole expected to happen. But sometimes things don't work out as expected.

Ralph Evinrude enrolled at the University of Wisconsin in 1926. During the summer, Ralph worked at the Elto plant and helped with the development of the soon-to-be-released Quad motor. At the end of his **sophomore** year of college, Ralph

generation: all the people born around the same time   **sophomore** (**sof** mor): the second year in high school or college

asked his parents if he could leave school "for just a semester" in order to see the Quad project through to completion. It turned out that Ralph, like his father, was more comfortable in business than in school. He never went back to the university.

While Ole's Elto business was zooming along, the old Evinrude company was lagging far behind. The company was sold again in 1925. It was sold yet again in 1928 to Milwaukee manufacturing giant Briggs & Stratton. This company made portable gasoline engines and parts for automobiles. Briggs & Stratton invested hundreds of thousands of dollars in the Evinrude plant but still couldn't make the company **profitable**. Stephen Briggs, president of Briggs & Stratton, got the idea to form a new group of **investors** to buy Evinrude from his company. The first person he approached was Ole

This man and woman caught lots of fish in their boat powered by an Evinrude motor.

profitable (**prof** i tuh buhl): making money   **investor**: a person who gives money to a business in hopes of making more money

41

PAMPHLET 92-846

The Evinrude Motor Company plant in Milwaukee, 1929.

Evinrude. Ole didn't have much to gain from buying into the Evinrude company. After all, Elto was doing very well and Evinrude was not. But he couldn't resist the chance to get back the company that bore his own name, not to mention Evinrude's fancy new factory. So Ole agreed, and in 1929, a new **corporation** was formed through the **merger** of 3 companies: Evinrude Motors, Elto Outboard Motor Company, and the smaller Lockwood Motor Company of Jackson, Michigan. The new company they created was called Outboard Motors Corporation (OMC). Ole was named company president. Stephen Briggs was named chairman of the board of directors. Ralph Evinrude took on the position

corporation (kor puh **ray** shuhn): a business that is organized legally   **merger**: when 2 or more companies join together to form a single, larger company

of **export manager** for the newly created corporation. The 3 companies would still be run as separate businesses, but all were really parts of OMC.

Ole and Stephen Briggs in 1929, the year they formed OMC.

The formation of OMC set the stage for a head-to-head battle with Johnson for control of the outboard motor business. But their timing could not have been worse. The year 1929 marked the beginning of the **Great Depression**. Many people had borrowed money from the bank to buy cars, homes, and other goods in the 1920s. But banks lent too much money. Prices fell. Banks failed. Factories closed, so many workers lost their jobs. Many people could barely afford to buy food and clothing. They stopped buying some things altogether, like outboard motors.

export manager: someone who oversees the selling of products to another country   **Great Depression**: the decade of the 1930s when many people in the United States had no jobs and were very poor

During the Great Depression, Evinrude tried making new products, including camping stoves and motorized bikes.

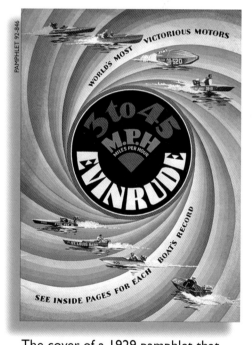

The cover of a 1929 pamphlet that called Evinrude racing motors the "World's Most Victorious Motors."

The company, already in **debt** from the merger, began to lose money quickly. With falling sales, Lockwood, the smallest of the 3 units that made up OMC, was closed down in 1930. In 1931 OMC managed to sell only a little more than 10,000 of its motors. **Wages** for the company's factory workers went down by about two-thirds. Factory hours were

debt (det): money that is owed to someone   **wage** (wayj): the money someone is paid for work

down to just 18 hours a week. Ole decided to give up his $25,000 salary in order to help the company stay in business.

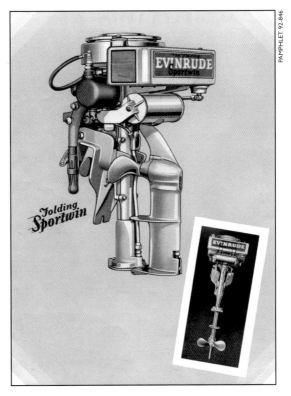

PAMPHLET 92-846

Another 1929 model was the Folding Sportwin.

In spite of these problems, Ole and his team continued to come up with new ideas. They knew the Great Depression would eventually end. They wanted to have the best motors ready for when that happened. In 1930, OMC brought out a new line of motors called the Fold-Lite. The Fold-Lite was the world's lightest twin-cylinder motor, weighing only 29 pounds. But more important, the motor could be folded up to the size of a suitcase. You could throw it into the trunk of your car or take it along on a train for an out-of-town vacation.

45

OMC sold only 10,291 motors in 1931, but Johnson's sales were falling even faster. For the first time, OMC became the biggest producer of outboard motors in the world. OMC kept the lead for decades.

In 1933, Bess's health, which had been weak for her entire adult life, began to fail again. This time, she was not able to bounce back. Bess died on May 13, 1933. Ole was **devastated** by his wife's death. His friends said he spent the next year drifting around in a lonely daze. He never recovered from the loss of the woman who had been his partner in business and in life. Ole died on July 12, 1934, at the age of 57. In less than a year and a half, the world lost the husband-wife team that first told the public, "Don't row!"

devastated (**dev** uh stay tid): very upset; destroyed

6

The Evinrude Legacy

After Ole's death, Ralph Evinrude took over as president of OMC. The loss of Ole was a huge blow to the company, but under Ralph's leadership OMC became profitable once again. OMC's chief rival, Johnson, had not come through the Great Depression as well as OMC had. By 1935 Johnson was **bankrupt**. Ralph Evinrude and Stephen Briggs decided to buy Johnson. They made it part of OMC. This new giant version of the company was by far the biggest producer of outboard motors in the world. Meanwhile, because of the success of OMC, many other outboard motor companies sprang up in Wisconsin and other parts of the

This 1939 Elto Cub weighed only 8½ pounds and was called the "world's lightest" outboard.

legacy (**leg** uh see): quality or character of something handed down from one generation to another
bankrupt: out of money and unable to pay bills

Midwest. Most of them are no longer in business, but for many years, Wisconsin was one of the most important producers of outboard motors in the world.

Some Important Wisconsin Manufacturing Companies

Wisconsin was a leader in manufacturing in the twentieth century.

Company	What They Make
Johnson Controls	Auto parts, building controls, batteries
S.C. Johnson	Cleaning products and housewares
Harley-Davidson	Motorcycles
Rockwell Automation	Robots for factory work
Kohler Company	Sinks, bathtubs, toilets
Briggs & Stratton	Gas engines
Oshkosh Truck	Heavy trucks and military vehicles

OMC made a lot of money during World War II from the sale of motors and other products to the military. Business continued to boom after the war, and many Americans were becoming wealthly.

Evinrude motors helped to transport soldiers and equipment during World War II.

People could now buy things that before had been **luxuries**, such as boats. By 1960, OMC was making nearly 400,000 outboard motors a year. They also made other products such as lawn mowers.

Ralph Evinrude led OMC until his retirement in 1982. By that time, the company had 9,000 employees and offices all over the world. Under Ralph's leadership, the company grew into a major manufacturer and

OMC made many products that had motors, like this Lawn-Boy lawn mower.

luxury (**luhk** shuh ree): something you don't really need but that you like having

49

an important part of Wisconsin's economy. Ralph himself became an important Milwaukee-area **philanthropist**. He gave money to many local arts and education organizations and hospitals. The Ralph Evinrude Foundation carries on that activity today. Ralph also married a movie star, Frances Langford. For many years, he was the owner of the Milwaukee Brewers baseball team. Ralph and Frances spent most of their retirement time in Florida. There they founded the Ralph Evinrude School of Marine **Technology** at the Florida Institute of Technology.

Ralph Evinrude showing off one of the company's 1954 models.

Ole Evinrude has been honored in many ways over the years. In 1981, the American Society of Mechanical Engineers honored the outboard motor

philanthropist (fuh **lan** thruh pist): a person who donates money to charities **technology** (tek **nol** uh jee): use of science to do practical things

as a National Historic Mechanical Engineering Landmark. An early Evinrude outboard is on display at the world-famous Science Museum in London, England. Ole has been honored in the Norwegian American Hall of Fame and the National Fresh Water Fishing Hall of Fame.

After decades of business success, OMC ran into trouble in the late 1990s. The company went bankrupt in 2000. The Evinrude and Johnson outboard motor lines were bought by a Canadian company called Bombardier

BRP US INC

Ralph Evinrude, with his movie star wife Frances Langford, was inducted into the National Marine Manufacturers Association Hall of Fame in 1989. This is the official portrait.

Recreational Products the following year. Bombardier continues to honor the Evinrude name by producing high-quality motors. Some of their business is still based in Wisconsin. These new motors have a lot in common with the original design that Ole Evinrude came up with 100 years ago. Although the technology has improved and the company has changed, Ole would still be able to recognize his outboard motor today.

A woman motors across a lake in a boat powered by an Evinrude Sportfour motor.

Friends enjoying a day on a lake in a motor boat.

Appendix

Ole's Time Line

1877 — Ole Evinrude is born in Norway on April 19.

1882 — The Evinrude family comes to America.

1892 — Ole builds his first boat and sails it on Lake Ripley.

1892–1899 — Ole works at various shops in Madison, Pittsburgh, and Chicago.

1900 — Ole moves to Milwaukee and works for the E. P. Allis Company.

1900–1908 — Ole forms a series of partnerships—including Clemick and Evinrude and the Motor Car Power Equipment Company—all of which fall apart quickly.

1906 — Ole gets his idea for an outboard motor while on a picnic.

Ole and Bess are married on November 21.

Cameron Waterman invents the first-known successful outboard motor.

1907 — Ralph Evinrude is born on September 27.

1909 — Ole builds and sells his first outboard motors.
Bess writes the famous "Don't Row!" slogan.

1911 — Ole forms the Evinrude Detachable Row Boat Motor
Company with Chris Meyer.

1914 — Ole sells his half of the company to Chris Meyer.

1920 — Ole and Bess form the Elto Outboard Motor
Company.

1929 — Evinrude, Elto, and Lockwood Motor Company merge
to form Outboard Motors Corporation (OMC), with
Ole as president of the new company.

1933 — Bess Evinrude dies.

1934 — Ole Evinrude dies.

Ralph Evinrude takes over as president of OMC.

1982 — Ralph retires from OMC.

2001 — Bombardier Recreational Products buys the Evinrude
motor line.

Glossary

Pronunciation Key

a   c<u>a</u>t (kat), pl<u>ai</u>d (plad),
h<u>a</u>lf (haf)

ah   f<u>a</u>ther (**fah** THur),
h<u>ea</u>rt (hahrt)

air   c<u>a</u>rry (**kair** ee), b<u>ear</u> (bair),
wh<u>ere</u> (whair)

aw   <u>a</u>ll (awl), l<u>aw</u> (law),
b<u>ough</u>t (bawt)

ay   s<u>ay</u> (say), br<u>ea</u>k (brayk),
v<u>ei</u>n (vayn)

e   b<u>e</u>t (bet), s<u>ay</u>s (sez),
d<u>ea</u>f (def)

ee   b<u>ee</u> (bee), t<u>ea</u>m (teem),
f<u>ea</u>r (feer)

i   b<u>i</u>t (bit), w<u>o</u>men (**wim** uhn),
b<u>ui</u>ld (bild)

ɪ   <u>i</u>ce (ɪs), l<u>ie</u> (lɪ), sk<u>y</u> (skɪ)

o   h<u>o</u>t (hot), w<u>a</u>tch (wotch)

oh   <u>o</u>pen (**oh** puhn), s<u>ew</u> (soh)

oi   b<u>oi</u>l (boil), b<u>oy</u> (boi)

oo   p<u>oo</u>l (pool), m<u>o</u>ve (moov),
sh<u>oe</u> (shoo)

or   <u>or</u>der (**or** dur), m<u>ore</u> (mor)

ou   h<u>ou</u>se (hous), n<u>ow</u> (nou)

u   g<u>oo</u>d (gud), sh<u>ou</u>ld (shud)

uh   c<u>u</u>p (kuhp), fl<u>oo</u>d (fluhd),
b<u>utto</u>n (**buht** uhn)

ur   b<u>ur</u>n (burn), p<u>ear</u>l (purl),
b<u>ir</u>d (burd)

yoo   <u>u</u>se (yooz), f<u>ew</u> (fyoo),
v<u>iew</u> (vyoo)

hw   <u>wh</u>at (hwuht), <u>wh</u>en (hwen)

TH   <u>th</u>at (THat), brea<u>the</u> (breeTH)

zh   mea<u>s</u>ure (**mezh** ur),
gara<u>ge</u> (guh **razh**)

accelerate (ak **sel** uh rate): to get faster and faster

agent (**ay** juhnt): a person who represents a business

apprentice (uh **pren** tis): someone who works for a set amount of time for low pay in return for being taught the skills of a trade

assembly line: an arrangement of machines and workers in which work passes from one worker to the next until the product is finished

associate (uh **soh** see it): a person involved in the company

bankrupt: out of money and unable to pay bills

blacksmith: someone who makes and fits horseshoes and other things made of iron

boarding house: a house that provides meals and rents rooms to live in

bookkeeping: keeping track of money

cabin cruiser: a type of boat with living quarters

carriage: a cart with wheels

compete (kuhm **peet**): to try hard to outdo someone at something

contraption (kuhn **trap** shuhn): a device or machine

corporation (kor puh **ray** shun): a business that is organized legally

custom: made or built to order

debt (det): money that is owed to someone

demonstration: a showing of how to do something

detachable (di **tach** uh buhl): a part that separates from something else

devastated (**dev** uh stay tid): very upset; destroyed

engineering (en juh **neer** ing): having to do with engines and engine design

entrepreneur (on truh pruh **nur**): a person who risks his or her money to start a business

export company: a company that sends products to other countries

export manager: someone who oversees the selling of products to another country

financially (fi **nan** shuh lee): having to do with money

forge (forj): a metal workshop

gadget (**gaj** it): a tool or part that does a particular job

generation: all the people born around the same time

Great Depression: the decade of the 1930s when many people in the United States had no jobs and were very poor

inherited (in **hair** i did): received a skill or quality passed down from parents

innovator: someone who invents something or does something in a new way

internal combustion (kuhm **bus** chuhn) **engine**: a type of engine in which fuel is burned inside an enclosed space in the engine rather than in an outside furnace

investor: a person who gives money to a business in hopes of making more money

lathe (layth): a machine that holds a piece of metal or wood while turning it against a cutting tool that shapes it

launched (lawnchd): introduced something new

legacy (**leg** uh see): quality or character of something handed down from one generation to another

57

luxury (luhk shuh ree): something you don't really need but that you like having

leisure (lee zhur): free time when you don't have to work

machinist (muh **shee** nist): somebody who makes, operates, or fixes machines

manufacturing (man yoo **fak** shur ring): making a product with the use of a machine

marketing: selling products or services

mechanical (muh **kan** i kuhl): having to do with machines

merger: when 2 or more companies join together to form a single, larger company

metallurgy (met uh lur jee): the science of working with metal

outboard motor: a motor attached to the outside of a boat

outdone: done better than

overwhelming: having a strong effect

partnership: a business agreement between 2 or more people

patent: (**pat** uhnt): a legal document that gives an inventor all of the rights to an invention

philanthropist (fuh **lan** thruh pist): a person who donates money to charities

plunged (pluhnjd): to move suddenly

portable: able to be moved or carried easily

profitable (prof i tuh buhl): making money

prospered (**pros** purd): to be successful

public relations: activities used to create a good reputation with the public

regain: to get something back

reputation (rep yoo **tay** shuhn): the opinion that people have about something or someone

revolutionary (rev uh **loo** shuhn air ree): a large, important change

rheumatism (**roo** muh tiz uhm): a painful condition of the muscles and joints

seafaring: working at sea

seasonal: happening during the spring, summer, fall, or winter

sightseer: a visitor

slogan: a phrase used by a business to sell something

sophomore (**sof** mor): the second year in high school or college

sorter: a person who arranges thing in groups

spectator sport: a sport watched by an audience

strict: making someone follow all the rules

technology (tek **nol** uh jee): use of science to do practical things

tinkering: making repairs without being an expert

touring car: a car made for driving long distances

venture: a project that could be risky

wage (wayj): the money someone is paid for work

Reading Group Guide and Activities

Discussion Questions

❖ Ole Evinrude was fascinated by boats all his life, and he fulfilled his dreams by starting his own outboard motor company to make it easy for other people to go boating. Even with good ideas, he had a hard time turning his good ideas into a successful product that people could buy. What kept him going? Why do you think he never lost sight of his goal?

❖ Most people today learn engineering and mechanical skills by going to school, but Ole Evinrude left school after third grade. He became an expert engineer by teaching himself the basics. He then learned a lot more on the job. What were some of the ways he had to educate himself? Why would it be more difficult today for a person who had left school after third grade to become a respected inventor, engineer, and designer?

❖ Ole started out working on his own, with only Bess to help him. What did they have to give up to make their business a success? To compare the Evinrudes' efforts with other people who started and ran successful businesses, read *Harley and the Davidsons* by Pete Barnes or *Tents, Tigers, and the Ringling Brothers* or *Casper Jaggi: Master Swiss Cheese Maker* by Jerry Apps. Then discuss whether you think the sacrifices were worth what it took to achieve success.

❖ After Ole and Bess died, how did their son Ralph continue his parents' success?

Activities

❖ Ole had a number of business failures before he got his outboard motor company started. Make a chart with 2 columns. On one side, list his business failures. On the other side, list the reasons why he failed. Then draw a line across the bottom of the chart and write the ideas that he had that finally made his business successful.

❖ Ole Evinrude started a successful company even though there were other companies that also made outboard motors. Make a time line of things he and Bess did to sell more motors while other companies went out of business.

❖ Bess Evinrude came up with the slogan "Don't Row" for her and Ole's motor company. Your group is in charge of creating a new commercial to help sell Ole's outboard motor. Write out what you will say and perform it for the class. Make sure you include a catchy slogan that will make people excited about Evinrude motors.

❖ Remember the story of how Ole came up with the idea for the outboard motor? While it may or may not be true, it is a great story. Make a series of comic strip-style drawings that show how Ole's invention went from idea to reality.

To Learn More about Innovators, Inventors, and Inventions

Barnes, Pete. *Harley and the Davidsons: Motorcycle Legends*. Madison: Wisconsin Historical Society Press, 2007.

Barretta, Gene. *Now & Ben: The Modern Inventions of Benjamin Franklin*. New York: Henry Holt and Company, 2006.

Busby, Peter. *First to Fly*. New York: Crown Books, 2002.

Byrd, Robert. *Leonardo: Beautiful Dreamer*. New York: Dutton Children's Books, 2003.

Garmon, Anita. *Alexander Graham Bell Invents*. Washington, D.C.: National Georgraphic, 2007.

Harness, Cheryl. *The Groundbreaking, Chance Taking Life of George Washington Carver and Science and Invention in America*. Washington, D.C.: National Geographic, 2008.

Lasky, Kathryn. *The Man Who Made Time Travel*. New York: Farrar, Straus, and Giroux, 2003.

St. George, Judith. *So You Want to be an Inventor?* New York: Philomel Books, 2002.

Steele, Philip. *Isaac Newton: The Man Who Changed Everything*. Washington, D.C.: National Geographic, 2007.

Thimmesh, Catherine. *Girls Think of Everything: Stories of Ingenious Inventions by Women*. Boston: Houghton Mifflin Company, 2000.

Wulffson, Don L. *The Kid Who Invented the Trampoline: More Surprising Stories about Inventions*. New York: Dutton Children's Books, 2001.

innovator: someone who invents something or does something in a new way

Acknowledgments

It took the work of many individuals and organizations to make this book possible and to make it something I am proud to have my name on. I am grateful to the people at Bombardier Recreational Products, particularly Christine Schultz, for generously granting permission to use a number of images owned by their company. Many of those images made their first public appearance in the book *Evinrude, Johnson and the Legend of OMC*. Its author, Jeffrey Rodengen, conducted a great deal of research on the life of Ole Evinrude, and I was fortunate to be able to use his book as a resource in preparing this publication. The same goes for Ralph Lambrecht's excellent article, "A Wisconsin Legend: Ole Evinrude and His Outboard Motor," which appeared in the Spring 2006 issue of the *Wisconsin Magazine of History*.

Above all, I would like to thank Bobbie Malone and Erika Janik of the Wisconsin Historical Society for their support and their tireless efforts at moving this project along—no small task given that they were working with one of the world's all-time laziest authors.

If this book inspires one kid somewhere out there to start messing around in the garage, pound on some metal, maybe glue some things together, and eventually come up with a new invention that is fun, useful, or both, it will all have been worth it.

Index

This index points you to the pages where you can read about persons, places, and ideas. If you do not find the word you are looking for, try to think of another word that means about the same thing.

When you see a page number in **bold** it means there is a picture on that page.